The Battles of Lexington and Concord

First Shots of the American Revolution

Stephen Whitwell

NEW YORK

Published in 2016 by The Rosen Publishing Group, Inc.
29 East 21st Street, New York, NY 10010

Library of Congress Cataloging-in-Publication Data

Whitwell, Stephen
The Battles of Lexington and Concord : first shots of the American Revolution / Stephen Whitwell. -- First edition.
    pages cm -- (Spotlight on American history)
  Includes bibliographical references and index.
  ISBN 978-1-4994-1722-7 (library bound) -- ISBN 978-1-4994-1719-7 (pbk.) -- ISBN 978-1-4994-1720-3
(6-pack)
1. Lexington, Battle of, Lexington, Mass., 1775--Juvenile literature. 2. Concord, Battle of, Concord, Mass.,
1775--Juvenile literature. I. Title.
  E241.L6W69 2016
  973.3'311--dc23
                                    2015014335

Manufactured in the United States of America

CPSIA Compliance Information: Batch #WS15PK: For Further Information contact Rosen Publishing, New York, New York at 1-800-237-9932

CONTENTS

COLONIAL ANGER AT GREAT BRITAIN

At the end of the 18th century, the king of Great Britain, George III, ruled the 13 American colonies. The colonists had become unhappy with his rule. They disliked the British soldiers who were sent to make sure that they obeyed the king's laws. The soldiers were known as **regulars**.

On March 5, 1770, a group of colonists in Boston threw snowballs at some British soldiers. The soldiers shot five colonists. This became known as the Boston **Massacre**.

British soldiers shot and killed Crispus Attucks on March 5, 1770. Attucks was the first American to give his life in America's fight for freedom.

This portrait of King George III shows him as a great hero. The American colonists did not think of him in this way.

King George III further angered the colonists by raising the tax on tea. The colonists would not stand for this new tax. The angry colonists stole tea and dumped it into Boston Harbor. This became known as the Boston Tea Party. The colonists wanted to make their own laws. At a meeting called the Continental Congress, they decided that the only way to do this was to fight the British.

THE BRITISH ARMY IN NORTH AMERICA

King George III sent Lieutenant General Thomas Gage, the commander in chief of the British army in North America, to Boston to become the governor of Massachusetts. Gage's job was to make sure that the colonists obeyed the law. Spies warned Gage that the colonists were gathering weapons to fight the British. The king ordered Gage to take the weapons away from the colonists. Gage knew that for this plan to succeed, it must be kept secret from the colonists.

On the night of April 18, 1775, Gage gathered 700 soldiers and prepared to march into the town of Concord, Massachusetts. Gage did not want the colonists to gather weapons that they could use against his soldiers. He sent patrols into the countryside on the night of April 18 to stop messengers from spreading the word about his actions. The colonists were not so easily tricked. They were ready for the British regulars.

General Thomas Gage was the commander in chief of the British army in America. Gage would fight against General George Washington soon after this portrait was painted.

PAUL REVERE AND SAMUEL PRESCOTT

Shortly before midnight on April 18, 1775, Paul Revere, a Boston silversmith, learned that Gage was planning to march from Boston to Concord. Revere arranged for two lanterns to be hung in a church steeple, where they could be seen for miles around. This was part of the colonists' plan to let neighboring towns know how the British would arrive. Two lit

This portrait of Paul Revere was painted by John Singleton Copley in 1775. Revere worked as a silversmith and engraver, but his most important work was as a patriot.

This illustration shows Paul Revere's famous ride of April 18, 1775. Revere rode 18 miles (29 km) to warn patriots that the British were marching to Concord.

lanterns meant the regulars were coming by water. One meant they were coming by land.

Revere then began an 18-mile (29 km) ride from Boston to Lexington and then to Concord. He wanted to warn the citizens about the regulars. Revere was captured on his way to Concord. A local doctor, Samuel Prescott, was able to warn the town. The weapons were hidden. A group of colonists got ready for a battle. These colonists were members of the **militia**. Some militia members were known as **minutemen** because they could get ready very quickly.

CAPTAIN PARKER AND HIS MINUTEMEN

At about 4:00 A.M. on April 19, 1775, Captain John Parker gathered 70 colonists to meet the British at Lexington Green. Parker was a local farmer with combat experience. Shortly before dawn, the British troops marched into view. Captain Parker ordered his men to **disperse** when he saw how outnumbered they were. As they were leaving, someone fired a

This color postcard shows the scene of the Battle of Lexington on April 19, 1775.

The minutemen of the American Revolution were volunteer soldiers. They were called minutemen because they could be ready for battle at a moment's notice.

musket. No one is sure from which side it came. Both sides began shooting at each other. By 5:00 A.M., the regulars had overpowered the colonists. Both minutemen and regulars were killed in the fighting.

The regulars continued to march the 6 miles (10 km) to Concord. The battle left the colonists with an important decision to make. They could return to their homes and **submit** to British rule. They could also choose to fight for their rights. They chose to fight. Captain Parker and his men left for Concord, where the battle would continue.

THE CAPTURE OF THE NORTH BRIDGE

The militia in Concord knew they were outnumbered by the British. At about 7:00 A.M., they decided not to defend the town. They retreated to a nearby hill overlooking the town. The British took control of Concord without firing a shot. They burned down the house where the colonists had hidden weapons. The fire from the house soon spread to the town hall. The militia saw the smoke and went back to defend the town. At about 9:30 A.M., the militia, who now numbered 450, reached the North Bridge. This bridge was one of the main entrances into Concord. A group of about 96 regulars stood guard there. No one knows who began to shoot first. Two colonists and three British soldiers were killed. The militia took control of the North Bridge. Killing the regulars was a very daring thing to do. The colonists had **defied** the king. The first shot that killed a regular at the North Bridge became known as the "shot heard 'round the world" because it changed history.

The fighting at the North Bridge left two colonists and three British soldiers dead. The famous American poet, Ralph Waldo Emerson, wrote about the fight at the North Bridge in his 1837 poem "Concord Hymn."

NEW RULES OF BATTLE

The militia kept arriving in Concord. The regulars decided to retreat when they realized that 2,000 colonists had gathered in the town. At about noon, the regulars retreated back down the 18-mile (29 km) route from which they had come. About 1 mile (1.5 km) east of Concord, the colonists attacked the regulars. In the 18th century, armies would line up on either side of a

This early 20th-century illustration shows British troops retreating from Concord. The colonists shot at the British as they retreated.

Many colonists had fought in the French and Indian War, during which they had learned to fight like Native Americans. This illustration shows how effective a smaller force could be.

battlefield to shoot at each other. The colonists did not do this. Instead they used fighting **techniques** that they had learned from Native Americans. They hid behind barns, trees, and rocks and fired at the British from all directions. They even ran ahead to shoot at the regulars as they approached. The colonists were not following the rules of battle. This angered and frightened the British. The British retreat turned into a run.

GENERAL PERCY AND HIS CANNONS

The regulars let out a cheer of relief when they reached Lexington at about 2:30 P.M. General Lord Hugh Percy, a British officer who had fought in many battles, was waiting for them. He had 1,000 British troops in battle **formation**, ready to fight. The general also had two cannons that he fired at the colonists, who were chasing the redcoats.

The cannon fire confused the colonists, who were not used to battle. They scattered to keep from being shot. This briefly stopped their advance on the regulars. The British used the break to get even for the **sniper** fire they had suffered since leaving Concord. The regulars burned houses and stole from people in Lexington. After the attack on Lexington, General Percy got his troops together for the 12-mile (19 km) march to Boston. British ships were waiting for them in Boston Harbor. Meanwhile the colonists had reorganized and kept shooting at the regulars.

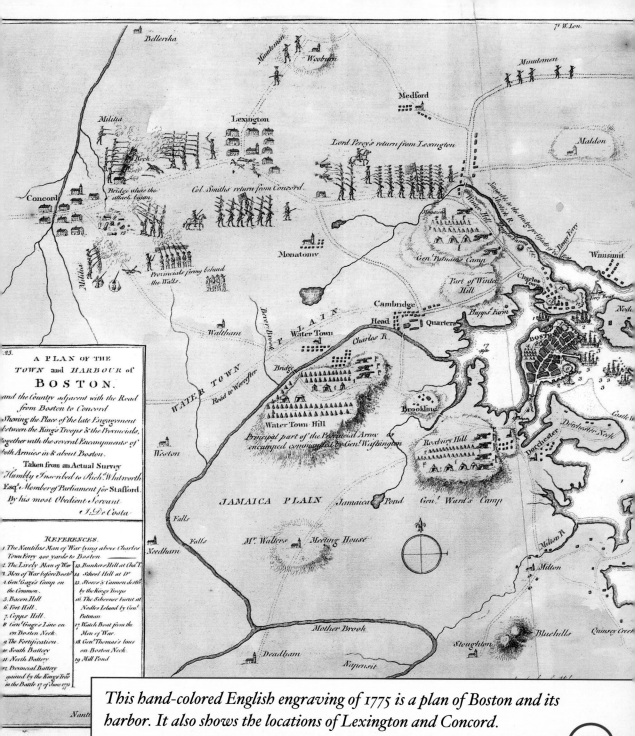

This hand-colored English engraving of 1775 is a plan of Boston and its harbor. It also shows the locations of Lexington and Concord.

MASSACRE AT MENOTOMY

The militia followed the regulars as they marched toward Boston Harbor. The militia formed a circle around the regulars and kept shooting at them. By the time they reached the town of Menotomy, the regulars were very angry. The colonists did not fight in the way the British were used to. Many of the regulars died, but the colonists were safely hidden. In Menotomy, the regulars burned houses, killing all of the people inside. Most of the women and children had been moved to safety already, but many people were killed.

The Retreat

From Concord to Lexington of the Army of Wild Irish Asses Defeated by the Brave American Militia
Mr. Deacon Mr. Leeings Mr. Halikens Mr. Bonds Houses and Barn all Plundred and Burnt on April 19.th

This engraving from 1775 celebrates "the Brave American Militia." It shows the British retreat from Concord to Lexington.

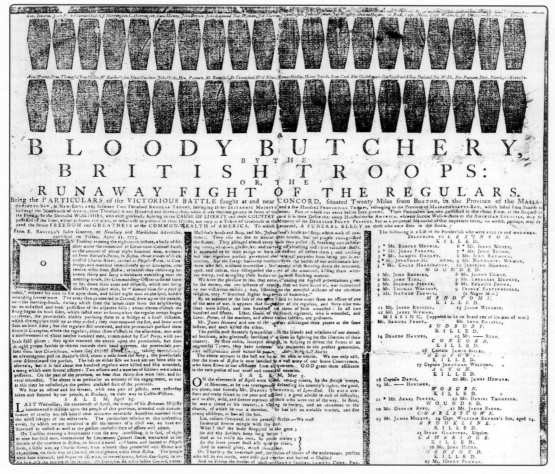

This 1775 broadside, or large newspaper page, reports on the American dead at the Battle of Concord. The coffins at the top represent the dead.

When the smoke cleared from the fighting in Menotomy, 25 colonists and at least 40 British soldiers were dead. What happened at Menotomy made many colonists think that the British were **savage** killers. As the stories about Menotomy spread, more and more colonists got ready for war with Great Britain.

THE DEAD AND THE WOUNDED

The regulars reached the hills of Charlestown, near Boston, after sundown on April 19, 1775. The colonists decided to stop their attack because they did not want to be shot at by the cannons on the warships. In Charlestown, the regulars got on small ships to go back to Boston Harbor, where larger ships were waiting for them.

After a day of fighting, the regulars had 73 men dead, another 174 wounded, and 26 missing. On the colonists' side, 49 people were dead, 40 were wounded, and 5 were missing. The colonists' losses were less than half of those suffered by the regulars. The battles at Lexington and Concord were finished, but the American Revolution had just begun. The day was a great victory for the colonists because they had proven that they could stand up to King George III.

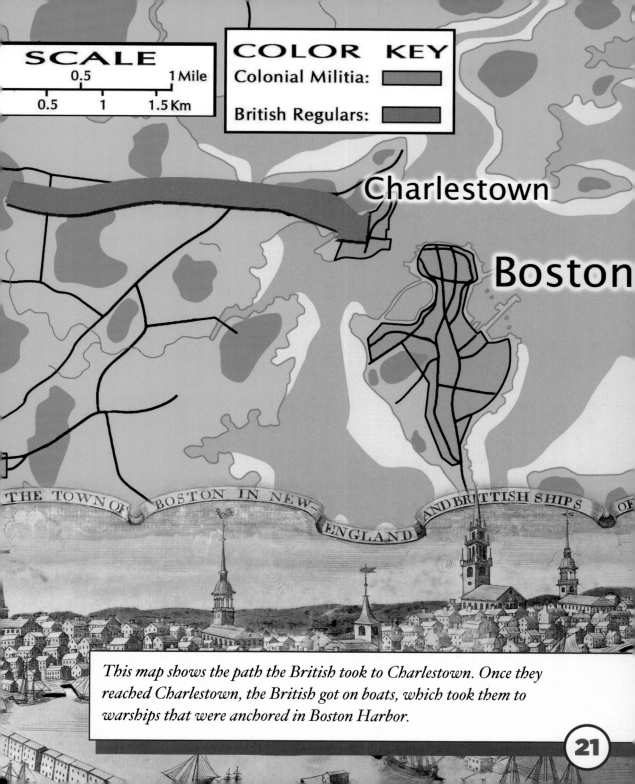

SCALE
0.5   1 Mile
0.5   1   1.5 Km

COLOR KEY
Colonial Militia:
British Regulars:

Charlestown

Boston

THE TOWN OF BOSTON IN NEW-ENGLAND AND BRITTISH SHIPS OF

This map shows the path the British took to Charlestown. Once they reached Charlestown, the British got on boats, which took them to warships that were anchored in Boston Harbor.

"GIVE ME LIBERTY OR GIVE ME DEATH"

Massachusetts was now officially at war with Great Britain. When news of the war reached the other colonies, more men arrived in Massachusetts to fight the regulars. Soon 16,000 colonists formed a half circle around Boston, trapping the regulars.

At first, some of the other colonies were doubtful that a war against Great Britain was a good idea. Patrick Henry, the first governor of Virginia, made a famous speech in which he said, "Give me liberty or give me death!" This speech **convinced** many colonists to go to war.

On May 10, 1775, leaders from every colony held a meeting to figure out what to do. They chose George Washington, a farmer from Virginia, to be the commander in chief of the colonial army. The colonists still hoped only to gain equal rights from the king. It would take another year before they would announce they wanted independence from Great Britain.

GLOSSARY

convinced (kun-VINSD) To have made a person believe something.

defied (dih-FYD) The act of having stood up to authority.

disperse (dis-PURS) To move or to scatter something in all directions.

formation (for-MAY-shun) The way in which something is arranged.

massacre (MA-sih-ker) Killing a group of helpless or unarmed people.

militia (muh-LIH-shuh) A group of people who are trained and ready to fight in an emergency.

minutemen (MIH-net-men) Armed Americans who were ready to fight at a moment's notice.

musket (MUS-kit) A gun with a long barrel used in battle and hunting.

regulars (REH-gyuh-lurz) Professional British soldiers.

savage (SA-vihj) Fierce, brutal, or cruel.

sniper (SNY-per) Someone who shoots at other people from a hidden position.

submit (sub-MIT) To surrender to the power, the control, or the authority of someone else.

techniques (tek-NEEKS) Special methods or systems used to do something.

INDEX

PRIMARY SOURCE LIST

Page 4: *Boston Massacre*, engraving, artist unknown, from *The Colored Patriots of the American Revolution: With Sketches of Several Distinguished Colored Persons: To Which is Added a Brief Survey of the Condition and Prospects of Colored Americans*, by William Cooper Nell (1816–1874). Published through Robert F. Wallcut, Boston, 1855.

Page 5: Oil portrait, *King George III,* created about 1762, by Allan Ramsay (1713–1784). The painting is at the National Portrait Gallery, London.

Page 7: *General the Hon. Thomas Gage* by David Martin (1737–1798). The portrait was created in 1775, a year after Thomas Gage became Military Governor of Massachusetts.

Page 8: *Paul Revere* by John Singleton Copley (1738–1815). Painted in 1768.

Page 10: Postcard created around 1906. Published by A. C. Bosselman & Co., New York.

Page 14: Engraving from *A Popular History of the United States, from the First Discovery of the Western Hemisphere by the Northmen, to the End of the Civil War; Preceded by a Sketch of the Pre-Historic Period and the Age of the Mound Builders*, by William Cullen Bryant and Sydney Howard Gay. Published by Charles Scribner's Sons, New York, 1890.

Page 17: *A Plan of the Town and Harbour of Boston and the Country adjacent' (with locations of the battles of Concord and Lexington, 19th April, 1775)* by J. de Costa. Engraved map was published in London, December 6, 1775.

Page 19. *Bloody Butchery By the British Troops, Salem 1775*, a paper released on April 19, 1775. It is housed at the American Antiquarian Society, Worcester, Massachusetts.

WEBSITES

Due to the changing nature of Internet links, PowerKids Press has developed an online list of websites related to the subject of this book. This site is updated regularly. Please use this link to access the list: www.powerkidslinks.com/soah/lexco